CHERELLE Z.

FACE IT
IT'S YOUR TIME TO THRIVE

6 STRATEGIES TO LEVERAGE YOUR LEADERSHIP POTENTIAL

Face It: Six Strategies to Leverage Your Leadership Potential

Copyright© 2020 Cherelle Z. Johnson

 Published by Final Step Publishing

P.O. Box 1447

Suffolk, VA 23439

www.finalsteppublishing.com

For Worldwide Distribution

Interior Design by Anno Domini Press

www.AnnoDominiPress.com

ISBN: 978-1-7342371-7-7

Table of Contents

FOREWORD

It has been said that life is a gift from God and what we do with that life is a gift to God. We all have been blessed with life, basic breath in our lungs, and also the faculty of mind to reason. Many people are caught up in chasing the American Dream or the pursuit of happiness. You know what it is, right?

- Work hard… play hard… pray sometimes

- Go to church once or twice a month, but especially on Christmas and Easter

- Buy a house, buy a car

- Get married, have kids, and have awesome friends

- Get likes on Facebook, Instagram, TikTok, or whatever the newest virtual reality of life (social media) is

- Make as much money as possible, be a boss

- And the list can go on

Our society naturally causes this gravitational pull to the life named above. We chase that carrot and end up on a hamster wheel of stress, success, failed relationships, and a laundry list of things we wish we would have done.

So, how do we get off the hamster wheel? How do we live lives that would be gifts back unto God? I believe what Cherelle Johnson has written in Face It is the key to moving you from mediocrity to maximizing your potential. It takes courage to maximize and utilize this life you have been given. The results of Facing Up to life's challenges and opportunities may not result in the American Dream, but it will result in you living the Dream that God has preordained for you. The giver of life has a plan for you, and each day you will be faced with a decision to live courageously or cowardly. Choose to be courageous today, and watch God open up doors that no man can close!

Cherelle Johnson takes us on a unique, easy flowing, inspiring, and instructional journey through the life of Queen Esther who started off as an orphan and rose to queen of a nation. Queen Esther took a stand that changed a nation, saved a people, and revealed God's favor.

Are you ready to move forward? Are you ready to maximize your obstacles? Are you ready to overcome years of being stuck on the hamster wheel of life? It's time for you to Face It.

INTRODUCTION

Leverage = To Use to Maximum Advantage

a "face" is a statement. It's what we look at when we're attentive. It communicates more than words. A "face" is at the forefront of our thinking. It's our primary source of rapid identification. Just as vital as our physical face to our body, is the courage it takes to *Face it*. The resolve to lead, the audacity to take a stand, the bravery to change and the boldness to hope beyond our current circumstances.

Some positions in life are given to us, while other opportunities are taken. Some individuals are born into an environment of strife, while others inherit success. Our world has had many micro-evolutions and revolutions that leave us begging for a revelation of truth. The story of Esther found in the bible depicts this very well. She was an orphan, raised by her older cousin, who became the queen of Persia.

I am sure the formula to becoming a queen was not in her situational DNA, yet there she was—a queen. Esther may not have realized she was destined to be a leader, but it was her time to FACE IT. Even after all the beauty treatments and being chosen as the queen, Esther still didn't quite understand her position. She went from being an orphan to becoming the queen of 127 provinces, from India to Ethiopia. And really, what did that mean and what was the point? I am not sure if her beauty preparations were equivalent to a modern spa day or more a glorified sex trafficking situation… What we do know, is that her position as queen was not her own.

From the King's perspective, her entire purpose was to please him; to be clean, pretty and sexually pleasing. At some point, even the superficial bragging rights from being chosen as the queen would get dated. It's interesting to me that years and years past this point (and I mean after Jesus-walked-the-earth years, and after women-went-to-work years, and even after work-from-home-CEO-mom years) sometimes we get caught in the same purpose trap that indicates your physical body is the main source of contribution.

It wasn't until conflict confronted her that Esther decided to mature from just looking *like* royalty to embracing her leadership inheritance. Esther was no stranger to conflict. Separated from her parents due to captivity and death makes for a trauma-filled life. Now this Jewish girl, hiding her true identity, had to make a decision.

> If you keep silent at this time, relief and deliverance will come to the Jewish people from another place, but you and your father's family will be destroyed. Who knows, perhaps you have come to your royal position for such a time as this.
>
> -Esther 4:14

Have you ever made your way out of something—an abusive relationship, poverty, or weight issues—just to be bombarded with that very conflict again? You are thanking the Lord for prosperity and, in that very place, He revealed the systemic roots to your past issue, and you can no longer live separate from what you thought was a singular conflict. It was in this space of conflict that Esther had to make a choice. The rules did not allow for her leadership inheritance, therefore in choosing to lead, she had to FACE it; she would become a martyr to her tolerable position and pursue God's purpose. This conflict was not a matter of choosing to live or lead. Esther had to recognize that to live, she must lead.

> Go and assemble all the Jews who can be found in Susa and fast for me. Don't eat or drink for three days, night or day. I and my female servants will also fast in the same way. After that, I will go to the king even if it is against the law. If I perish, I perish.
>
> -Esther 4:16

Leadership has many colors and has been defined by many gurus. I believe a leader is one who uses their influence for an eternal perspective. The spheres of influence can look very different. Your placement may be with your potty-training toddler, PhD colleagues, or co-workers. Regardless, you must FACE it.

After fasting, Esther dressed herself properly, stood on her platform and prepared to move forward. It was at this point that she embraced her character, unveiled her confidence and utilized her competence.

Her decision to FACE it, opened the door for God's power to move. She had favor with the king and exposed a plot to commit genocide against the Jewish population. After she FACED it, she moved from being *a* queen to *the* queen.

> It was at this point that she embraced her character, unveiled her confidence and utilized her competence.

Her position did not change at all, but the significance of her role was vastly different. She was clean, pretty and sexually pleasing, while serving as a lawyer, legislator and co-commander of the providence. She not only replaced the previous queen, she redesigned the role of queen. Often, it is not until our true character, confidence and competence are aligned that we can accept our leadership inheritance and make bold contributions.

Esther is not on the who's who list of top national leaders, but her courage and humble tenacity has shaped my philosophy of leadership itself. I often speak with individuals about their gifts, purpose and pursuits and have found a common block to forward movement, the unidentified self. Confidence, character and competence are three major themes in this book, and I believe that my life is a continual testimony to how they affect our uniqueness and success.

I believe we have been robbed of our confidence, in a spiral of degrading character and dismissing our competence as trivial matters. This discrepancy is seen biblically, socioeconomically and personally. Unfortunately, the consequence of this design is a people bursting with potential, but never emptied. Full of dreams, yet only awake to what's seen and unanswered. This bursting potential turns toxic towards its own body if kept leashed and eventually weakens others who come close.

I hope that this book becomes the eulogy to your untapped potential. My goal is to equip you to leverage your leadership potential and live a life directly facing all your dreams, desires and destinations. Living unapologetically can feel like an unsolved mystery as we mature and experience more and more life. At one point, you think you've figured yourself out only to find out there is more. FACING it is not a destination, it's a checkpoint in life. Periodically, we need to look in the mirror directly to confront blemishes, treat the irritated skin, or simply apply the substance necessary to maintain flexibility. No matter your stage in life, embracing the six strategies presented in this book will release your inheritance and leverage your leadership potential.

This book is written to those who feel stuck and are ready to level up. This is for the less-than, marginalized, abused and forgotten. This serves as your thirty-day notice to confront your fears, take responsibility and expose your skills and strengths. My prayer is that this ministers to your soul and serves as a launching pad for your thriving identity. By the Grace of God, you will go beyond and be the leader God created you to be as you *FACE it*!

FIX IT

Correcting the Confidence Gap

*All the royal officials and the people of the royal provinces
know that one law applies to every man or woman who
approaches the king in the inner courtyard and who has not
been summoned—the death penalty—unless the king extends
the gold scepter, allowing that person to live. I have not been
summoned to appear before the king for the last thirty days.*

Esther 4:11

*a*utomatic correction can be a blessing or a curse. The feature known as AutoCorrect is designed to improve our writing by correcting errors we make as we type, but what is considered an error is based on a list of common errors. If you are typing an academic paper, drafting a contract or some other professional document, it is very useful. If you are sending a text message to your friend and the use of slang words is imperative for making your point, AutoCorrect can get in the way. Spelling and grammar were never my strong point, so I've had more appreciation for the feature than not, but every now and then it gets in the way. For example, my name is spelled C H E R E L L E. Without reprogramming AutoCorrect either changes the spelling or squiggly lines my name. While I know there are rules, sometimes there are exceptions based on context. I found "AutoCorrect" under the "Tools" tab and customized the list by adding or deleting words so that the feature would work better for me. Did you know that the list although preset, it is not permanent? I believe that we not only type with this feature, but we live with this feature in our mind. The world has a list of common errors and suggestions for correction that does not always produce efficiency for our leadership capacity. It is imperative that we take a maintenance day and reflect on our programing to make sure it is best reflective of us. To FIX it, is to repurpose the AutoCorrect. It suggests taking the time to examine what is happening in your soul and aligning it with what you desire your life to communicate to the world.

Esther's response to the issue presented by Mordecai was on autocorrect. She basically said, everyone knows this law… but she had not yet adjusted her autocorrect list to reflect the exception of the king extending the golden scepter to spare her life. When reading chapters 1-3 of the book of Esther, it outlines hardship but also highlights the favor she had with the king. There was even a moment where she reported a conspiracy to the king on the behalf of Mordecai before and the outcome was successful (Esther 2:21-23), so what was the issue now? How was this different? I believe it was time for her to leverage her competence by updating her confidence gap.

> So don't throw away your confidence, which has a great reward. For you
> need endurance, so that after you have done God's will, you may receive
> what was promised.
> -Hebrews 10:35-36

When I was in third grade, my mom decided to move to West Point, VA. This wasn't a far or distant location. It was about 40 minutes from our current location in Virginia's capitol city, Richmond. This was a bittersweet move for us, harder on my mom and brother than me. My mom was raised in West Point and had no plans of returning. She grew up during the 60's and had clear memories of what it was like to be among the first black students to integrate high schools. She never imagined her children would finalize their secondary education walking the same halls. My brother, who is six years older than I, was a budding athlete with professional potential, excited to enter high school and play football for an elite team. While my parents were not managing life together well, my mom had to make a major decision. For my brother while his athletic skills were being fostered, his educational opportunities weren't. The middle school we were districted for was just horrible. If fact, it didn't exist much longer after we moved. I had not too long before transferred from private school to public school as well. My parents couldn't afford the tuition for both of us to attend a suitable school, so amidst other personal parental decisions, we moved to West Point.

I was an excited and happy kid. I had no real feelings toward the move as a third grader. I loved school. I was very familiar with the town because of spring breaks with my Momma Lucy (my grandmother), October crab carnivals and November oyster festival during the visit to Aunt Ann's house. My first day at

West Point Elementary School was fascinating. I went from a classroom of thirty kids to a room of about twelve. I was one of three black girls in my grade and my gym teacher's name was Mrs. White. The irony was that she was the only black teacher in the elementary school, and before moving, I had never had a white teacher or peer.

With all these modifications, what impacted me the most was one negative comment. It was as if these words were the code for a bomb of low self-esteem to implode in my soul. As a new student, it was suggested that I start coming to *"after school"* with my teacher. It was a time for instructors to spend more individualized attention with students as needed. I remember sitting with the teacher and several other students asking the question, "Why am I here?"

"Because you're not smart" was the response from James, a fellow third grader.

"You are not smart" translated to me as "you are not good enough." I remember it so clearly because that phrase became an anthem for me all the way to senior year in high school.

When I was in middle school I was unaware that I had made the honor roll for the very first time until someone else pointed it out to me. After that, my mom said I had to continue to keep my grades up, and she gave me money for every "A" I earned. Somehow my mom seemed to know that one of my top five strengths was competition, so the money motivation worked. I studied and become an A student.

A few years later while selecting courses for my senior year, one of my best friends, Amanda, challenged me to take all advance level classes. She had always taken every AP, dual-enrollment, "extra-smart-person" class that the school had to offer. The only class we had ever taken together was PE. I replied, "Amanda, I am not smart enough."

"Says who?" she responded.

At that point I was embarrassed to admit that a little boy named James who wasn't even around past elementary school had said it. West Point had a very small public school system. I basically went to school with the same people from third grade until I graduated with a class of sixty-two. So I replied, "Mrs. Chestnut already has my classes picked."

"You can change your schedule, and you should take dual enrollment English with me," Amanda said. Now, I am sure I laughed at her because that translated to me as, "you are smart." With this reverse bullying, I finally changed my schedule to include four advanced level courses and graduated with great success! When I changed my class schedule, it also seemed to change the narrative I accepted about myself. I took the harder course, still afraid yet confident. In that season my confidence gap didn't close, but I began a quest to narrow the space between God's truth and anything else.

> What then are we to say about these things? If God is for us, who is against us?
>
> -Romans 8:31

Starts & Statues

A gap is the distance between what should be happening, and what is happening. Our confidence gap is the difference between how we act and what we think or believe. The goal is to have our actions align with our beliefs that are rooted in truth. The bible is our anchor to truth. Without it we tend to climb the ladder of influence negatively, adopting "inaccurate beliefs based on selective observations, false assumptions and misguided conclusions" (Kegan & Lahey). Our confidence should reflect a strong belief about what's true. To lead well, we must first address any confidence gaps, followed by identifying the "starts" and the "statues."

The story about James identifies the starting point of my confidence gap when I distinctly experienced an internal alteration of identity. Theses initiators or "starts" can derive from something seemingly innocent. Identifying starts for most of us will take us down memory lane to elementary school.

> Failure is like a statue that is tangible but not living; it is not your reality.

For some, what introduces our confidence gap is a failure. Failure is like a statue that is tangible but not living; it is not your reality.

On the campus of James Madison University, right before the crosswalk, is a life-sized statue of none other than James Madison himself. This statue has the name of a real historic icon and is carved in his image. We take pictures with it, decorate it during homecoming, and stop at it to tell stories and share memories. No matter how we regard this statue, it is not living. It does not reproduce anything for us. It's simply a place of reference.

Many times, in life we fail at something and instead of analyzing it, we idolize it. I believe it's healthy to admit failure, but it should not have creative rights to the rest of our life. Failure, no matter how painful or embarrassing, only has the power you give it. To "FIX it" we must give ourselves (and perhaps others) permission to live beyond those circumstances and celebrate becoming.

To "Face it" and leverage your leadership potential, it's imperative to evaluate how you feel about your abilities with what you believe about God. Once we are impacted by Christ, we get a chance to reexamine our true selves and partner with the only author and finisher of our faith. Being born again presents the possibility of living authentically as designed, not just standing still. As we meditate on His word, we can apply eternal truths to our present situations, and fix the hindrances that kept us on a mediocre growth track. After identifying our starts and statues, we must correct our confidence gap with our belief, speech and perspective.

> After identifying our starts and statues, we must correct our confidence gap with our belief, speech and perspective.

Royal Perspective

> For I am persuaded that neither death nor life, nor angels nor rulers, nor things present nor things to come, nor powers, nor height nor depth, nor any other created thing will be able to separate us from the love of God that is in Christ Jesus our Lord.
>
> -Romans 8:38-39

Confidence is related to action and our ability to succeed. Self-esteem is the value you give yourself. We can be confident in our ability, but not believe it has value in the world. We can also be confident in one area of life and lack confidence in another. Working out (producing endorphins and higher testosterone levels), dressing better, power poses. or talking about something you know well may contribute to an increased confidence level. Healthy confidence is a major element for anyone to leverage leadership potential. Healthy confidence believes "If God is for us, who can be against us." My natural "feel-good" chemicals can be off the charts, but ultimately, my confidence is fueled by belief in God.

> Death and life are in the power of the tongue, and those who love it will eat its fruit.
>
> -Proverbs 18:21

Have you ever tried to count calories? MyFitnessPal is a great diet and fitness tracking tool that determines the optimal caloric intake and nutrition for the user. By scanning the bar code on the food item, or typing in its name, it provides information about the food entry and how its nutrition correlates with the other items tracked for that day.

Have you ever tracked your words? Have you ever stopped to submit the phrase you were about to say through an application that keeps track of your optimal speaking impact? In other words, have you ever had to tame your tongue? My husband introduced me to book titled "The Forty-Day Word Fast: A Spiritual Journal to Eliminate Toxic Words from Your Life" (Charisma House, 2015) by Tim Cameron. Not only does this fast help track our words, but it helps us to eliminate toxic words that we are saying to ourselves or others. It even considers your thoughts and the intents of your heart. I considered myself a well-mannered communicator but after completing the Word Fast, I discovered many growth opportunities. It's not that I said bad words, rather my thoughts were not always life giving for myself or others. I found corners where my words did not align with truth, or where I wanted to foster change. It's hard to grow as a leader when within your own sphere you don't sound like a leader.

Words are so powerful yet can have zero impact on our souls. Like calories, the right ones can be energy for endurance, while empty words can feel good at the moment, but make you feel heavy later. Face it, to close a confidence gap, we must speak well. If you want to change the direction of your life, change your language toward yourself.

> But you are a chosen generation, a royal priesthood, a holy nation,
> His own special people, that you may proclaim the praises of Him who
> called you out of darkness into His marvelous light.
> -1 Peter 2:9

Viewpoint is another key element of leadership. Leaders should communicate their vision well and function with a royal perspective of themselves. Having a royal perspective means to view yourself as a queen. How your view yourself should be that of royalty, knowing that your heaven father does. Now, I am not saying that leaders should be the movie version royalty-meaning not relatable, rude and rich. But perspective plays a major role in our spheres of influence. Sometimes the image of the leader is portrayed as the one who stands alone; however, I often identify leaders with an arsenal of support. When Esther had to "FACE it," she requested that all the Jews as well as her maidservants fast. She didn't approach the king without their support.

Every leader needs a support, such as a midwife. A midwife is a health professional who cares for mothers and newborns during childbirth. Once it is confirmed that the woman is pregnant, the role of the midwife begins. Similarly, when we are ready to leverage our potential by first doing some soul searching, it is vital to have proper support for birthing this new level of capacity. We all need someone to help us labor. The beauty about finding individuals to support you is that, nine times out of ten, their involvement on your behalf will sharpen their own confidence and personal productivity. Having a royal perspective causes one to make decisions beneficial for a legacy. Thinking higher of yourself, regardless of your circumstance allows you to have long term vision for your life and as a result, make decisions that help others coming behind you. Your viewpoint with a position of royalty, and not simply routine and rules, will activate your leadership inheritance and leading will become a mandate. Correct your confidence gap by making decisions as royalty, and become the true version of self-wealthy, empowering and premier.

Let's Chat:

Reflection Questions

1. What personal (self-governing) laws are you living by when you should be living as the exception to those laws? In other words, what are the "AutoCorrect" words or deeds that need to be added to, or deleted in your mind, thoughts and feelings.?

2. "Failure is only a statue; it is not your reality." Identify statues in your life that need to be repurposed or removed. Take time to analyze the functions of failure without idolizing those feelings.

3. When investigating your gaps, identify their "starts." If you are holding on to any negative words or thoughts toward yourself as a result of an experience, write about the situation and its impact on you. Find a scripture that confirms truth about you and rewrite the situation or list with that truth. (See the chart for an example.)

Suggested	Truth
You are unintelligent	
You are unattractive	
You are not loved	
You are insignificant	

FAITH IT

Believe Beyond

*Now without faith it is impossible to please God, since
the one who draws near to Him must believe that He
exists and that He rewards those who seek Him.*

Hebrews 11:6

*H*ebrews 11:6 is my son's life scripture. A life scripture is a bible verse that specifically speaks to your purpose. Christopher Jr., whom we affectionately call Chip, says that Noah is his favorite bible hero. Green is his favorite color and the song *Good Good Father* by Chris Tomlin is his favorite song. At a tender age, the boy was already full of absolutes. My son is a genius and I am still discovering all of what that will mean for his future. His life verse, and frankly the only scripture he had memorized, has changed my life. Although the words were very familiar to me, I had never dug deep until his exploration.

One day Chip, three years old at the time, was eating a delicious red apple with me. I took the first bite (we call that "taxes" in our home) and gave the rest to him to finish. We were outside on a somewhat cloudy, calm day. Chip had planned for me to be the one to eat the skin of that apple and he would eat the inside. I wanted the apple anyway and could bite larger chunks than just the skin of the apple, so I agreed. As he ate to core, he noticed that there were seeds inside. Now, Chip is the epitome of an internal thinker and processor. This means that he has an internal discourse that we may have no clue of until it is seen in action. I was grateful to notice this in him early so I could curtail our relationship. I've learned to be patient with his actions allowing them to interpret his thoughts for me. I saw that he had turned his attention to the seeds and was no longer interested in eating at all. I watched as he gathered each seed, found some dirt and buried the seeds. It was so precious. When he finished, he came to me and said,

"Mommy, I hope it rains soon." He never explained his thoughts or even asked for another snack. It didn't matter that we were at an amusement park in the middle of the day with friends- he was now fixed on the rain. He had no concern for anything else than what he knew could happen with this application of seeds in the ground and water. In his preschool class, he had been taught all about apples and this was finally his opportunity to participate in what he had learned.

This cute moment reminded me that astounding outcomes are often produced with applied faith, not just accepted faith. Accepting Jesus sustains your eternity, which is the substance of our hope, while applying Jesus propels your immediacy, resulting in evidence. We accept that fact that apple seeds produce apple trees and we reap the ultimate benefits of juicy apples. But until you've planted your own tree or have witnessed the process, your evidence is still borrowed. The blend of acknowledgment and application is what it takes to "Faith it." Even when the circumstances seem troublesome or incomplete, apply what you understand to be true, and allow God's nature to produce a harvest in your soul that is sweet and plentiful. Faith can be a tricky subject to teach a child, but I hope my son is rooted in this truth forever.

> What good is it, my brothers and sisters, if someone claims to have faith
> but does not have works?
> > -James 2:14

To explore any true leadership potential, calling or trait, it takes faith; the compete trust in something. I would suggest that it takes a simple understanding of "the faith" as well as the complexity of applying faith. Christian faith is a conviction that we were created by God in His image with a destiny He designed for us. Most people believe God exists and many agree that Jesus Christ is God. They would call on no other name than Christ. They have enough understanding of "The Faith" for salvation; Jesus is Lord and Savior. The complexity in that statement is when we must trust what we believe in day-to-day situations.

> Go and assemble all the Jews who can be found in Susa and fast for me.
> Don't eat or drink for three days, night or day. I and my female servants
> will also fast in the same way. After that, I will go to the king even if it is
> against the law. If I perish, I perish.
> > -Esther 4:16

Esther demonstrated her faith when she fasted. She asked all the Jews as well as her servants to fast for her. This was her "Faith it" moment and the preparation for her to "FACE it." Biblical fasting is a discipline of abstaining from food for spiritual purposes. Discipline in its simplest form is training towards a desired result even when the future outcome is unknown. The discipline cannot predict the exact outcome, but it can produce an "even if" resolution in your soul. The primary purpose of fasting is to fix our hearts on Jesus. It reminds us of the things that control us and that we are sustained by the word of God. Fasting is mostly a private matter, but in this case, Esther initiated a corporate absolute fast (no food or drink) because she realized that this was a matter of national emergency. She was about to embark on something beyond herself and her generation and therefore needed to apply her faith in an extreme manner. The goal of any spiritual discipline is to decrease your personal dependency and to stir up (or train) your faith in what's unseen, yet desired.

This moment is so vital and speaks volumes for Esther. She likely had not fasted since she first began to live in the palace. Esther had been an orphan, raised by her cousin Mordecai who instructed her keep hidden her Jewish ethnicity, especially from the Persian king.

There may be seasons of our journey where we need to put aside our origin for greater exposure. Now, I am not saying that you are to be someone else or downgrade your cultural lineage. I am mainly referring to part of your culture norms that is not as significant to your purpose in that season.

"There has never been a female to do this…"

"Black women just don't…"

"Tall girls shouldn't wear…"

"A Christian woman does not…"

Virginia born and raised women. I am from a middle-class family of four and grew up in a rural environment with very little diversity of people groups with a mentality of scarcity. I am a first-generation college graduate from a matriarch-led family. This information about me is vital to my identity but does not reflect my destiny at large. My husband always teaches that your origin in addition to your destiny denotes your identity. Many times, we only associate our identity with our origin alone. If our youth or past was traumatic, it can be hard to believe beyond those themes. Our core beliefs start to take root within those experiences, possibly blocking our vision for more. Therefore, it is key to reconcile our identities with biblical truth and individual purpose. Esther had to endure a lot up to this point, and yet she still strived for what she had not yet seen.

Now faith is the reality of what is hoped for, the proof of what is not seen.
-Hebrews 11:1

Ultimately, to declare this "even if" disposition, Esther had to transition from a fact-driven mindset to a faith-driven one. Similarly, a "Faith it" disposition causes us to shift our mindsets from Scar-City to Dream City**.**

Faith on the Move

As we explore our confidence gap, we can often see the segment of our life where a lack of faith has taken residence. It's usually in that gap where we see complacency, possibly even masked as efficiency. Some of us can see years of choices which have taken roots on that confidence gap.

I've always had big dreams. I could see potential in anything and envision big things for it. I love executive coaching for that very reason. I love to hear someone's heart and help lead them towards their greater selves. But when it came to myself, I often let my origin and limited exposure scale down my dreams. I could always see big but didn't always *do* big. I reached a point where my scarcity mentality began to dictate my view of God. It was so subtle. I thought I was just being practical and calculated when truly I was living with fear. I was afraid to try things or ask for something because I only pictured "one." I only gave myself one chance, one opportunity or one option. I only worked within one gifting, strived for one theme and liked one style. My portion of life was limited.

As scriptures began to transform my mind, I began to embrace the possibility of "more than one." One day, while working out on the elliptical exercise machine, I was reading a book by Valorie Burton titled "Listen to your Life". That day I was in a funk. I felt scatter-brained and frustrated. I desired to position myself in one lane of my life, but God had shown me many lanes. I wanted to know if I should completely commit to building our church or building a business. Should I homeschool my kids or enroll them in a public school? Should I focus on increasing my cooking skills or completely pursue my coaching desires? As I was reading this book, I found my legs were no longer moving on the machine. Suddenly it was so simple and clear to me. The answer was, YES. Yes to all of it. I didn't just have vison for a moment, but I would experience these dreams over some time. What I am doing at this moment is not my ONE thing, it is one of many things that would add to my multifaceted dream. I suddenly could hear unhindered similar to how we can hear better after our ears pop while flying in an airplane or driving in the mountains. I can hear without the fog. The same sounds.

"Believing beyond" is a decision to relocate your soul and "FAITH it." I had to "FAITH it" and not just believe in abundance in terms of what God can provide, but also abundance in how God can demonstrate through me. God wanted me to see His vastness in peace, comfort, and opportunity. From then on, I've had to switch my residency from Scar City to Dream City where the motto is *"Now to him who is able to do above and beyond all that we ask or think according to the power that works in us."* (Eph. 3:20)

Although I have not moved too far in terms of physical distance, it seems I now live on a new planet. I have lived in the same state for more than thirty-three years. Moving to a new area requires us to learn new physical and social territory, adjust to new climate and traffic patterns, while possibly facing language barriers. It takes intentional work to re-settle in a new city, but many people endure this transition because of the opportunities that they hope to gain. When you can relocate your soul, you learn that there is another economy that's reflective of faith. In this system, giving makes you wealthy and purging adds. You start to view money as a seed and not your source, while generosity becomes your objective and demonstration of who you have faith in. Moving from Scar City to Dream City changes your perspective from "What does this city have for me?" to "What do I have that contributes to this city?" Scar City was gripped with fear and lack, while the landscape of Dream City is filled with possibility and abundance.

Believing Again

When preparing to move, we need to pack, purge and make an announcement. This process can be exciting or horrifying. I think of it as an opportunity to organize. Similarly, when your soul relocates, we must pack and take with us all the vision, dreams and healthy habits. Taking more than what we'll use, would be hoarding and antagonistic to generosity. Generosity is a key element to your abundance living. Generosity is a demonstration of faith while hoarding is a demonstration of fear. In Dream City, we cannot grow what we do not sow. In other words, your giving will be the GPS of your gaining. The potential for more hinges on what is planted and where. In the process of moving our soul, let's increase our discipline of giving. This is a secure way to make the announcement of your move and secure new ownership in your soul. One of the hardest moves that my husband and I made was relocating to our current home, which I love so dearly. This house is in the same city as our previous home, only about ten minutes away. It has the perfect capacity for our growing family with the curb appeal I wanted. It's even made with red brick just as my daughter desired: one minute from the elementary school, centrally located neighborhood, with a rising resale value. With our desires met, this was still the hardest move. Five years prior to this relocation, we were equally content with a move to another home that did not end favorably.

One year after our wedding I was pregnant with our first sweetheart and looking to purchase our first home. It was an exciting time. We had completed Dave Ramsey's *Financial Peace University* course, paid off debit and saved up the funds needed for a down payment. I was proud of our stewardship of our one income, and just knew this house was for us. It was for sale by its owners, and how my husband met them seemed so divine. They agreed to do a lease-to-own contract with us while we were gathering the necessary paperwork for the mortgage. Unfortunately, the mortgage process took an unforeseen turn and the lease-to-own contract ended before we could settle on a closing material. To this day, we cannot pinpoint the exact problem but it was not a lack of resources. We still have the very clear memory of moving out of what we thought was our first family home.

Our first major move did not end as expected and the highest hurdle I had to jump was the faith to believe again. I didn't realize the damage to my faith until a new opportunity came for us to look for a home. I had no desire to move. I was very grateful for the townhome we were renting. Others around us were moving and buying homes with seemingly little effort. My husband and I led many house blessing ceremonies and believed with others for their new home. We were full of faith for others, but fear slept on our doormat like an old harmless hound dog with the floppy ears. We even had the audacity to move our church into a new building seven times the size of our current facility and with hopes that the congregation would participate in a capital campaign to secure the loan. Finally, we felt that it was time for us to look for a house again. To believe again felt like rehabilitation. We had to "FAITH it" and believe beyond the scar of tragedy. We had to work our faith muscle for ourselves this time. It was like watching a toddler learn to walk. There were a couple of falls, but ultimately, we had to celebrate each small step and refocus our faith along the journey. Many times to FAITH it involves a relocation of your soul and a switch from being a renter to an owner. There's more responsibility when you take ownership of your dreams. This could include negations, down payments and closing cost, yet the investment in the legacy you build has profitable sustainability that releases your leadership capacity.

I am sure you can relate to the temptation of complacency. You won't even apply for the new job because last time you applied they said you were too inexperienced. The blind date was a waste of time, so you won't attempt to give the random smiling face at the coffee shop the time of day. Maybe you've become so accustomed to a toxic relationship that your hope for reconciliation is non-existent. That dream of writing a book seems so unrealistic that you don't even journal as you use to. Maybe the death of a loved one still has you unsettled with life, or the sudden decline in your heath is a hindrance. Here's the truth:

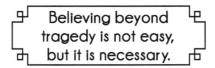

Believing beyond
tragedy is not easy,
but it is necessary.

Whatever it is, wherever it is, let's serve an eviction notice to fear and the ordinary today. It's time to make the announcement to yourself that your current location is no longer suitable for the leadership potential that's boiling in your heart. Let's decide to "Faith it," to apply our faith, again and again.

I believe the speech by Esther's cousin, Mordeci, that begins: "for such a time as this...," is the very locker room speech that the Lord gives us when He wants us to reveal our authentic selves. Sometimes we must silence the distractions and do a soul search. Regardless of what was prior, she entered a new moment to make a decision, using her influence. To truly lead, Esther had to FAITH it. She had to believe that there was more to her purpose as well as more discovery of self. She had to view herself as an abundant person. When she declared the fast, she was making a statement of faith. She revealed her origin as a tool for her destiny. She encouraged her entire culture to draw near to God for what was ahead of them. Instead of letting the them get killed by what they didn't know, she leaned on what they already knew to gird strength-faith in God. The facts were written. *"One law applies to every man and woman who approaches the king in the inner courtyard and who has not been summoned-the death penalty."* But what was also written was a hope *"...unless the king extends the gold scepter allowing the person to live"* (Esther 4:11). Fasting indicated that she believed in something that was not yet seen. She held onto the hope and not just to what was visible.

Let's Chat:

So how do I know if I am living by faith or not? How do I know the difference? I asked this same question trying to grow my garden. We must give more attention to motives and be more intentional with our actions. When I moved to a new home, there were garden beds already in the backyard, so I decided to plant produce. I failed but I learned that a seed is meant to reproduce in the appropriate soil and atmosphere. What I thought may have been produce was really a weed. I had a great soil for seed development, but what I didn't consider was the affect of the harsh atmosphere. I quickly learned, that to recognize the difference, I needed to spend more time grooming the garden.

Reflection Questions

1. What does generosity mean to you? How can you demonstrate generosity toward others?

   _____

   _____

   _____

2. What things or experiences are you hoarding? How could these be hindrances to relocating your soul?

   _____

   _____

   _____

3. In what way(s) do you need to demonstrate your faith? Where do you need try again?

   _____

   _____

   _____

Action Steps to Faith it

1. Prepare: Starting on Monday, do not eat lunch for the next 5 days. During the time you usually eat lunch, spend time praying for your next level.

2. Purge: Think about that closet, shed or basement that is full of "just-in-cases" or "what-ifs." Plan a day to purge the unnecessary materials and items. Allow this to be your active step toward removing hoarded fear from your domain.

3. Provide: Pick an individual, group or organization to demonstrate generosity toward. In the next seven days, make a financial contribution (above your normal comfort) and journal about your experience of increased generosity.

> For this very reason, make every effort to supplement your faith with goodness, goodness with knowledge, 6 knowledge with self-control, self-control with endurance, endurance with godliness, 7 godliness with brotherly affection, and brotherly affection with love. 8 For if you possess these qualities in increasing measure, they will keep you from being useless or unfruitful in the knowledge of our Lord Jesus Christ.
>
> -2 Peter 1:5-8

FACE IT

Accept responsibility

*On the third day, Esther dressed in her royal clothing and
stood in the inner courtyard of the palace facing it.*

Esther 5:1

*E*veryone comes to a point in their life, a crossroad, where a decision must be
made. Some decisions are made subconsciously due to our routine of life or
core beliefs. Decisions to eat a snack, check Instagram, get the mail, read a book,
wash your face, ask the barista for light ice in your keto Frappuccino are often
made without much effort or thought. Then there are the times when saying "yes"
or "no" to one situation feels like jumping off a cliff with no bungee cord on a
cloudy day hoping that the green light you visualized indicating "go ahead" was
not really blue or controlled by Satan or actually translated "go home."

When I discovered that it was time for me to "Face it," I made the decision
to have professional photos made. I know it may sound trivial, but for me it was
a major decision because I realized that my disregard for professional headshots
were in direct correlation with the downplay of my own value. As an author,
entrepreneur and instructor, I had to accept responsibility to amplify my own
voice and proclaim that I am a professional, not an imposter.

Speak up

Leadership is about influence and movement. There are thousands of books
about leadership, biblically and secularly, but ultimately, I believe that leadership
is an inheritance. Some inheritances are simply passed down because you are an
heir and it is a matter of order. Just because of your position in the system (family
or organization) your inheritance is a matter of receiving. Other times, you are a

leader because of your characteristics. You were born this way regardless of who you seem to be connected to. Your environment and social constructs play a large role in how this is seen, but leadership is indeed your theme. To me it doesn't matter how you came to this resolve, rather what you do with it. To *FACE it*, we must accept responsibility and journey towards the dream. Titled or not, liked or not, prepared or not, to leverage our influence, we must jump off our cliff of comfort and control into a free fall adrenaline rush of passionate trust and fortitude.

The opportunity to lead is an honorable one and presents itself in many forms. In the biblical narrative, there is a story about five daughters who shows us what it means to *Face it* by asking for their inheritance.

> They stood before Moses, the priest Eleazar, the leaders, and the entire community at the entrance to the tent of meeting and said 'Our father died in the wilderness, but he was not among Korah's followers, who gathered together against the Lord. Instead, he died because of his own sin, and he had no sons. Why should the name of our father be taken away from his clan? Since he had no son, give us property among our father's brothers.'
>
> —Numbers 27: 2-4

Now it's one thing to inquire about something that is lawfully yours, but it's another to ask for something that could be yours, but was not designated to be yours. These daughters were not just asking for an opportunity to be seen, they were asking for property or land which represented provision for their identity and destiny. This reads like a simple question they asked but denotes so much more.

In the context, usually a land inheritance goes from the father to his son. A woman generally received a dowry from her father as a wedding gift and typically, the father required his potential son-in-law to provide much, if not all that dowry. A dowry might consist of clothes, jewelry, money, furniture or more, and it was thought that the dowry could help provide for the woman if her husband left her or unexpectedly died. This was the social norm until these daughters spoke up and presented brand now perspective.

Their suggestion was faith-filled, innovative and revelatory; all distinctive of a leadership leap.

Their request was not bound by the current facts. The property inquired about was not even available yet. They hadn't seen it because they hadn't reached their destination. Canaan was the settling location of the promised land and their awareness of God's promise gave insight to this potential inheritance. The fact that they stood and asked for it exposed their leadership potential and their strategy denoted their capacity.

Because they were making a bold request they needed to be intentional. The girls could have pulled Moses aside and spoke with him individually, but it was vital to be in front of the priest Eleazar, the leaders, and the whole congregation. After the request was granted, some time had passed, and Moses was no longer the leader when it was time to divide and distribute the actual property. The daughters could now recall *"The Lord commanded Moses to give us an inheritance among our relatives"* and have the witnesses and support of the others to implement this inheritance (Joshua 17:4). I am impressed with their team-oriented leadership style. They stood before the community, all together and with one vision. It is not easy for five individuals to agree on any approach and do it well. For the sake of the values and vision, they had to stand together. Often, even when it seems we are standing alone for a cause, we are usually commencing a legacy of unity for co-heirs of this inheritance or promise.

When the daughters made their request, even their proximity at the entrance of the tabernacle of meetings seemed strategic. Their positioning and posture indicated humility and respect for the current leadership. A humble leader has a balanced desire for God's order and success. I might have interrupted the meeting fussing at the men in charge, saying how rude they were for not considering poor me when making decisions. Many times, we exhaust our efforts fighting just to be heard, instead of seizing the opportunity to speak truth. We place the battle externally rather than integrally, causing one to emphasis the minor details, missing the big picture. The daughters could focus on the big picture despite their leadership title or lack thereof. Without having a distinguished role at the meeting, they could be assertive while avoiding both passivity and aggression in their approach. Living a life of integrity has its sacrifices in our competitive market, but it creates a smooth launching pad for assertiveness during confrontation and when it matters the most.

Moses brought their case before the Lord, and the Lord answered him, 'What Zelophehad's daughters say is correct. You are to give them hereditary property among their father's brothers and transfer their father's inheritance to them. Tell the Israelites: 'When a man dies without having a son, transfer his inheritance to his daughter.'
-Numbers 27: 5-8

Their leadership capacity was seen in many ways. One being their ability to influence the governing leaders to lean on the Lord's guidance and change the law. These girls ignited change for the future of many. They jumped at an opportunity to receive an inheritance that no law was set towards prior to their request. They had a vision of something that had never been pictured before. It was bold and risky, but the potential for success was worth it. What's most notable is that the Lord said yes! Moses did not have a systematic solution for them. The creator of the heavens and earth had to intervene to properly address their bold request.

To FACE it, we must speak up strategically (at the right time, in front of the right people) and from a place of integrity. Integrity lives at the crossroad where honesty meets consistency, and personal integrity provides the infrastructure for promotion. Some of us need to look inward and accept responsibility for our professionalism, while for others, it's time to amplify your voice. So, what are you waiting for? Is it time for you to speak up? Or live a life tethered to the truth of God's word that speaks for you? Are you willing to accept responsibility at work that positions you for the promotion? Do you need to boldly ask for a pay raise? Is it time to make an investment to develop your skills, or are you ready to reach out and offer your expertise?

Don't Give Up

Have you ever become tired of waiting for a breakthrough or a switch in prospective? Have you ever resolved in your heart that the best decision right now would be to quit?

Every year, I tell my husband that I am going to quit something (and I am never talking about carbs and sugar). It's usually my nonprofit organization, my career as a college instructor, a woman I'm mentoring, or even mothering. I think to myself, "I quit!"

When I was pregnant with my third child, I remember threating to quit everything during the first trimester while experiencing moderate nausea and extreme exhaustion. The week after I found out we were expecting I was scheduled to take a prerequisite course for a for a PhD program. It seemed to be the worst time to be attending a course in person, five days a week, three hours a day for four consecutive weeks with men and women who were at least eleven years younger than I was. I had to master sixteen weeks of curriculum within a four-week time frame. Every single day, while doing my homework, I would tell my husband that I was going to quit. His response every time was, "Just give it one more day." Somehow, despite my feelings, I gave it one more day for the next four weeks and excelled in the course.

Galatians 6:9 states: *"Let us not get tired of doing good, for we will reap at the proper time if we don't give up."* Our relationship with *quit* has a lot to do with your ability to thrive. To survive means to continue to exist, while thriving indicates a flourishing and prosperous situation, especially despite unfavorable circumstances. If you are at the point of giving up, the good news is that you are in the right place. It is usually at this point that we begin to truly thrive. Without affliction, we would be just surviving. During opposition we see our true potential and can step up to the plate and thrive as leaders.

To FACE it, we need to make a shift. For me, the shift was a mindset adjustment. Instead of surrendering to the intimidation of all that was happening at large, I had to focus and commit to what needed to happen next. For some, that shift is a complete 180-degree lifestyle change. While for others, particularly you who are reading chapter 3 of this book, the movement may look more like a 90-degree pivot towards purpose. Thriving begins at that point where we decide to pivot towards purpose. It is when you make a strategic change in your life that becomes the anchor for you next bold moment of success. And although purpose looks different for many, it requires endurance for all.

We always have a choice whether to survive (continue) or to thrive (flourish). The difficultly is that it is not always clear how each choice will resolve. Esther was also at this crossroad in life. She was faced with a opportunity to survive at status quo or thrive at a risk. Could it be that her whole life was preserved for this moment? When Esther aligned with her true identity as a child of God, she was able to see her greater purpose. Her preparation was no longer based on her fleeting outward beauty but rather on her inward spiritual growth. She could not wait on a solution because she was the solution. We cannot not give up at this point because we are the answer and there is a harvest wait for us to reap!

Dress Up

On the third day, Esther dressed in her royal clothing and stood in the inner courtyard of the palace facing it. The king was sitting on his royal throne in the royal courtroom, facing its entrance.
                                                                    -Esther 5:1

Most of us have heard the saying "dress for success." Esther had to wear her royal robe as a reminder of the platform God had given her to approach the king. Members of the armed forces, first responders, and members of other organizations while in uniform suggests a level of authority and purpose without him or her saying a word. They do not need to explain where the authority comes from, where they were trained or why. Esther had to put on her royal attire before proceeding. She no longer questioned if this was really her robe to wear or if it still belonged to the previous Queen. She didn't even have to wonder if it was her style, she simply needed to wear it. As a leader, you not only have to dress your external, but your soul and sphere also. Your soul is the immaterial part of you that is directly affected by your spiritual desires. Your sphere consists of the material life around you which is impacted by your spiritual life. Oftentimes, how you dress is often an expression of how you feel about your inward identity

Moses was no stranger to this concept of Face It. He saw God's power and provision during his leadership journey, but it came to a point where he had to ask for more of God's presence. He needed to know that the presence of God was with him, otherwise there was no value to the journey. He didn't just want to see change; his desire was to experience change. If what you are moving towards requires total dependence on the Lord as well as an intimate experience with the Lord, you may be *Facing it.* Moses asked for something he couldn't even humanly handle. Because he *faced it,* by asking *"Please, let me see your glory"* (Exodus 33:18) *"We all, with unveiled faces, are looking as in a mirror at the glory of the Lord and are being transformed into the same image from glory to glory."* (2 Corinthians 3:18).

Let's Chat:

Facing it, is not a subconscious act. It takes an intentional choice and can be accompanied by opposition and unfamiliarity. What opportunity do you need to move towards? How can you pivot towards your purpose? Let me suggest some questions to ask yourself that may help discern your next decision:

1. Does it require God's presence?

2. Does it suggest a revival within?

3. Could its impact last beyond you?

Action: Get dressed and Take a Stand

1. For one week, keep track of the opportunities you may have missed. For example, I was grocery shopping and wanted to complement someone, but I didn't. At the end of the week, reflect and discuss how you can seize an opportunity in the coming week.

2. Identify one area or situation in your life where you want to quit. Tell a friend, and together, agree on a plan to thrive in that area for the next ninety days.

3. Headshots send a message and are the new calling card in the world of digital identity. Treat yourself to a mini-makeover, and schedule to have professional photographs taken after reading the book, I know your true identity will be clear and you will feel brand new.

FIND IT

Define Your Dream

Lord, my heart is not proud;
my eyes are not haughty.
I do not get involved with things
too great or too wondrous for me.
Instead, I have calmed and quieted my soul
like a weaned child with its mother;
my soul is like a weaned child.

Israel, put your hope in the Lord,
both now and forever.

Psalm 131

I am so grateful for growth in the Lord. When I look back over my life, I get tickled thinking about the outcome and results of my decisions. Psalm 131 read like a breath of fresh air when I was at a recent retreat. When I read it, I just paused and looked around slowly. It was as if I were in a movie and at this scene someone cued the epiphany music (with a soft trumpet melody and subtle cadence). The room seemed too quiet, and the words began to crescendo in my heart. I was full of gratitude because this verse was a true soundtrack in my life. I know this to be true because I also had a clear memory of the contrary years prior. Looking back, I would describe myself as proud. I thought it was my passion for justice and my ambition, but honestly, my viewpoint was immature and fearful.

Clarity

Have you ever walked into a room, welcomed in by a very strong smell that you couldn't identify? The fragrance seemed to only exist at your point of entry. This may have been a good experience or a horrible one, but nonetheless, it was distinctive. You know you smell something, but either you can't name the fragrance or you are not sure where it is coming from. That's what it feels like when you walk in a room with a large capacity for leadership, yet it is undiscovered. Your presence or impact screams a significant statement; we just don't know why or how to define it. That fragrance was me, a woman with robust leadership capacity, yet we could not quite put our hands on what it was in the moment, we just knew when it was present.

In 2012, a couple sponsored a trip for my husband and me to visit a church and campus conference in Johannesburg and Cape Town, South Africa. This was six months after the launch service of our church plant, three months after I graduated with my master's degree and two months after learning that my womb was hosting its first disciple. Up to this point, I had already had an exciting faith journey and major growth opportunities and yet there was more. I thought I had experienced the caterpillar to butterfly stage, but really, I had only come to terms that it was time to start the cocoon. This trip to South Africa was life-changing and an experience that birthed a new season for my life. While there we attended conferences and services, met and connected with amazing leaders, received great affirmation for the ministry we were leading back home; and just felt loved. In the midst, the Lord was opening my heart for great deposits from Him.

"Do not defend your opinion, defend the Gospel."

This statement was a lesson I was learning then, and that I still must remind myself from time to time. The Lord took me all the way to South Africa to tell me this. I am a very opinionated individual, so instinctively I had many… opinions about this. I was in a season of life where I felt it was necessary to clarify my roles and show meaning to my positions.

You see, I was a stay-at-home wife with two lucrative degrees, married to a bi-vocational church-planting pastor. This place in life was as foreign to me as it was being in "Jo'burg" singing a worship song in Zulu. What I was doing felt right, but I had no trained language to describe it. I had no title or official position in our church, but I was doing many things. Chris and I decided before marriage that I would be a stay-at-home mom for the early years, but I had not yet birthed children. We had a small glimpse of the partnership we were building in ministry and business, and it was important that we set a firm foundation of harmony in our home. Therefore, at the time, we chose a single income lifestyle. This would allow us to travel together and freely make decisions as needed. We sacrificed a few financial opportunities. But most of all, it was my soul that needed some grounding. One of the toughest things for me to settle with was the value of my contributions.

Now don't get me wrong, I loved the freedom and autonomy over my day. I made a project and time slot out of everything. I was so busy doing stuff that Chris had to kindly ask why his stay-at-home wife was out of the home as much as he was. I loved being my husband's assistant at church, mentoring women over lunch and having the time to actually enjoy preparing dinner at home. It was only uncomfortable when I had to explain me to other people. The question "What do you do?" would always leave me tongue-tied.

"Oh, you work for the church?" Well no, I am a full-time volunteer like everyone else including my husband.

"Oh, you're a stay-at-home mom?" Well not a mom yet; we plan to be.

"Oh, you're the First Lady…" Um, please don't call me that.

I could not quite get my story down enough for a self-satisfying response. I was on the bridge between what I was doing and who God was calling me to be. I knew in my heart that I was a leader, but to me, I didn't look like one. It was during those thoughts that the Lord drew a very clear stop sign in my mind and instructed me to stop talking… "Do not defend your opinion, defend the Gospel." The more I grew in my understanding of God, the less concerned I was with my own impact. It was *His* impact that was worth defending. It was *His* title that needed to be properly addressed and defined in my own heart. With this change of heart, when people pitied me for being the wife of a pastor, instead of defending my role and value, I could hear beyond their question and address their negative view or lack of exposure. It was then that I could illuminate God's purposes through my experience as a pastor's wife. I, myself, once had a less-than-desirable view of the *poor lil'* pastors' wives. It wasn't until my exposures changed that I was able to view God's design. Oftentimes, we can't Find it because we are busy defending what we don't want it to be.

(Un)Discovered

> A woman approached him with an alabaster jar of very expensive perfume. She poured it on his head as he was reclining at the table. When the disciples saw it, they were indignant. 'Why this waste?' they asked. 'This might have been sold for a great deal and given to the poor.'
> -Matt. 26:6-9

I am not sure if this woman knew the influence of her actions at the time, but we know it left a great impression with Jesus. The disciples, Jesus' closest friends, were bothered by her actions because they were unaware of its purpose. But Jesus knew, and affirmed and defended her. What the disciples said seemed very true and practical, especially when there were other current clear needs to be met. This pure act of honor produced an impact that would memorialize her. In doing this, she also honored the Lord in ways that she wasn't even aware of. Jesus, knowing that the others were bothered, responds by explaining *"By pouring this perfume on my body, she has prepared me for burial"* (Matt. 26:12). This means that although men were confused, He was honored that she would participate in his earthly mission which was soon approaching.

Sometimes, we can't wait for permission, an invitation, or approval from others when we are living undiscovered. As long as we are affirmed by God, defining our action will be His pleasure. To "Find it", we must refocus and take a different view of our current situation. In *The Practice of Adaptive Leadership*, Heifetz and Linkey refer to this as "getting on the balcony". This mean getting some mental distance between you and a situation to get a bigger picture and gain perspective. Jesus knew what was going to happen to him, even if the woman with the perfume did not. He always has a bigger perspective. Jesus was a carpenter's son and at the same time, the Lord of Lords. He was aware of the system He was committed to saving, while never forsaking the future kingdom that dwelled within. The woman never had to defend herself because Jesus does not have to discover someone He designs.

As soon as I gave up my right to self-identify by my uncertainties, I found my authentic self, and I liked her too. *It* was right there with me the entire time. I was growing content being a multi-faceted dreamer. I settled in the fact that I can do many different things and have many passions that didn't minimize my uniqueness. Being undefined by others allows you to define yourself. Because we are usually outlined by our situations, organizations, or the roles we play, we are often defined by "that one contribution" or "that one situation" when we are multi-faceted dreamers. We don't just have one dream we probably have a few dreams that are motivated by key characteristics that make up your identity. It is easy to forsake the "multi" in us because it seems arbitrary and blurry at times, but I believe God designed us this way to keep us thirsty for the future He has in store for us. As a multi-faceted dreamer, you have an anatomy or a system to be considered without apology.

Esther was more than the beauty treatments she had, more than a physical delight, more than a replacement for pleasure. Although she held the esteemed title of Queen, that did not define her leadership capacity. No longer let your title in life define you as a leader. You, the leader, should define the title.

Dream Anatomy

Have you ever found yourself asking these questions: "I know what I do, but is that who I am? How does who I am inform what I do?" I found that the best way to categorize oneself is by your relationship with the creator. When the Lord becomes your resource for identity, your question changes to "When should I go?" You ask fewer clarifying questions and more directional ones. You settle with the thought of being an available vessel and stand dressed for your next movement.

As a vessel, like the body, there are many components that contribute to who you are and what you do. I believe that every dream has an anatomy and once you organize your sphere, you can organize your dreams and desires in a way that leverages your leadership capacity. This refreshing reality turns every situation into learning opportunities resulting in increased exposure of self.

Often, passion is what kick-starts the new project, social involvement or job hunt. Passion is what motivates us to FACE it, but it is not always the mode we depend on to sustain us. Mission refers to the "what" of your dream. Skills are tools we use to accomplish the mission. Your skills can often depict the HOW of your dream. Skills can be natural talents or developed talents. If you know your mission, that can encourage you to enhance a non-natural skill to better accomplish the mission. If you know your skills, they can also help paint the picture of your mission. We can share similar skills and missions as someone else but have a different vision. Your purpose is the vision of your dream. It's the "why" of the dream? The purpose is the end goal. When we are settled on our why, it will cause us to grow or accommodate for any lack in skill and passion. You can use the dream anatomy to organize the big picture of our life, or to keep you on focused on your day to day living.

Self-awareness is a key indicator of maturity. When you are leading, how you define yourself will be your distinctive. How you view self can truly set a lasting impact for your future opportunities to FACE it. The ability to spend time *being*, rather than just *doing*, will illuminate your dream anatomy. This is when we see the pure expression of our identity. So often our confidence comes from clarity that gives us the energy to make great contributions. But sometimes, the confidence in what I can see, excludes that courage I actually need to navigate who I can become.

Defining your dream anatomy is more than a clear title or position. It's your moment to express the structure and internal working of what makes YOU. It's at this point when your soul becomes like a weaned child, meaning your focus "ripens" from what you need, to who needs you. Your responses and reactions will produce more than clarity, but an impact on the world around you that affects unborn generations.

> So often our confidence comes from clarity that gives us the energy to make great contributions. But sometimes, the confidence in what I can see, excludes that courage I actually need to navigate who I can become.

> 'What is it, Queen Esther?' the king asked her. 'Whatever you want, even to half the kingdom, will be given to you.'
>
> -Esther 5:3

Growing as a leader, you have to FIND It. You must discover and own who you are and defend the "it" that illuminates truth. I thought I had to define myself to others to gain the respect to be me. But really, defending the Gospel of Jesus Christ did all the defining I needed. My defense was not only with words, but rather with deed. As my life better aligned with His commands, then people not only experienced me, but the presence of the Lord. When people encountered Jesus, His fruit was obvious. Some defined Him as healer because they experienced His healing power. Others called Him teacher because they were taught and transformed. I am not saying that you must be God, I am saying to let the fruit of the Spirit flow unhindered in your life and your reputation will proceed you.

Let's Chat:

Reflection Questions

1. Who or what do you defend the most? Does that defense prove itself productive? Why or why not?

_____

_____

_____

2. Which excites you more: Talking about your title or talking about your experiences?

_____

_____

_____

3. Name and explain areas in your life where you have clarity, but lack courage to grow?

_____

_____

_____

4. Identify your dream using the chart below:

Question	Dream Elements	Your Response
What excites me?	Passion	
What do I do well?	Skill	
Who do I want to impact?	Mission	
What do I want to give to the world?	Purpose	

FINESSE IT

Express Your influence

If I have found favor in the eyes of the king, and if it pleases the king to grant my petition and perform my request, may the king and Haman come to the banquet I will prepare for them. Tomorrow I will do what the king has asked.

Esther 5:8

*A*fter fasting for three days, Esther put on her royal attire and stood in the inner courts to be seen by the king. The king extended the scepter as she had hoped and granted her such favor that he was willing to give her even half the kingdom. She could have unloaded all her information on him at that moment, letting him know that Haman was going to kill her people. Instead, she invited him and Haman to dinner. It seemed anti climatic for the weight of the moment. They came to the banquet and she, yet again, invited them both to another banquet. Why didn't she just spill the beans at the first banquet? Maybe she wanted to make them comfortable with her, to gain trust. Maybe she was giving Haman an opportunity to show his wickedness himself. She may have hesitated because she had two mysteries to unveil, Haman's plot as well as her true identity as a Jewish woman. Regardless, I admire how Esther brought the situation to her courts. I honestly think she just had to do what's necessary to handle the situation her own way that would honor God.

One of the most mentally obstructing things for me is when I am asked to do something that, when I watch others do it, I can't. At least I can't do it the way they did it. I get so focused on how they are doing the *thing* rather than the desired outcome of what's being done. To leverage your leadership potential in these circumstances, we use the art of finesse! *Finesse* is a fun word for me to say and a term referring to the skillful handling of a situation. As a leader, we must express our influence strategically, which calls for us to FINESSE it.

In many situations I did not act with finesse and it was stressful. Some people have absolutely zero strive towards finesse. I know you've been in that situation before, right. You felt so bad for how something was handled that you just had to say a kind word to help fill the empty hole left by the anti-finesser. I've found that when situations seem to be anti-finesseable, the culprit is a lack of preparation and a rushed life. A Finesseologist would not be hindered in that way. They would suggest accomplish the outcome in a way that does not burn bridges needed for future collaborations. This is what separates leading from managing. Managers maintain a system, while leaders design new, sustainable ones. Innovation is sometimes a lost art, but as leaders, it is necessary. Esther didn't initially create something new when she hosted a banquet. In fact, the previous queen was hosting a banquet for the women right before she was kicked out of the kingdom. Esther, using her finesse started by hosting a banquet that resulted not only with the desired outcome, but with her in charge of the wellbeing of her extended family. Esther, like Vashti, did not follow the King's orders, but I believe that she was spared due to preparation, patience and her previous reputation of having favor with the king.

Have you ever wanted to do something practical in a moment, but stopped because it didn't seem "epic" enough? Honestly, I've withheld ideas because in my mind they did not seem important. Sometimes we should act on those practical or careful measures using our strength, perspective or resources to contribute to a moment. A quality finesse-er has patience in each moment with vision for *the* moment to come.

Order

The first way to prepare for your certificate of finesse is to live a life of order. Sometimes we need to simply organize our lives to see our lives. Our living environment can speak volumes about our season, our disposition or our strengths. If you are looking to get to know yourself better or increase your proficiency, pay attention to your spaces including your vehicle, bedroom, closets, office, etc. The lack of order or significance might be indicating something about you. It will be hard to finesse anything if you have low regard for your own.

I must admit that I not only flourish in an organized environment, I love to do the organizing! My physical surrounding indeed shows my strengths. I am a strategic planner and organizational science nerd. If you in no way enjoy organizing, you can start by simply decluttering. Everyone can use a good purge occasionally. Research has shown a link between our healthy habits and the neatness of our home. When our living space is disorganized, we tend to feel anxious and overwhelmed. According to psychologist Sherry Benton, PhD, disorganization hinders efficiency with simple tasks we do daily such as eating, getting dressed, driving, etc. Now, we all can see why this is true, but our homes, offices, and bedrooms sometimes reflect otherwise.

After you declutter your space and mind you should then live and lead within your new-found capacity. This was another lesson I learned that same year I traveled to South Africa for that first time. This lesson was just as tough because I thought leading was a narrow gift, but the Lord was showing me otherwise. Five years' prior (2007) to this visit, my life looked completely different. I was a junior in college and had experienced a serious growth spirt in the Lord. I was very active in college ministry and truly living for Jesus like never before. At that time, I was confident that I had an administrative gift, therefore, appropriately so, I help start the admin team. Up to that point, what I had seen as "administration" was more like a planner, organizer and logistics thinker. Those things came natural to me. One night I had a very vivid dream and the Lord showed me that administration was more than a natural talent to organize paperwork and schedules. For me, an administrative gift would produce spiritual strategy in leadership and that I would put people in order, not just things. For me, this was literally like "the handwriting is on the wall" moment. With this increased vision, I soon began to adapt how I lead in my sphere.

Fast-forward five years, while visiting SA, I was at another shaping moment. Like I said in the previous chapter, rapid growth and change would be an understatement to describe this season, and yet there was so much more to learn. As I was spending time writing and reflecting, I had another mind blowing, life-changing moment with the Lord as I overlooked the beautiful landscape of Cape Town. Days after getting the message *"Do not defend your opinion, defend the Gospel,"* I was getting names of individuals who I had access to, yet I was not optimizing my leadership influence with. The next encouragement I received was to systematize my leadership capacity in order to reach more people and start with my current circle of friends. Another light bulb turned on in my heart and mind as this imprint was confirmed multiple times by leaders who just met me and had no natural context for my influence. Another wow moment, this time with my husband as a witness. I committed to, what I called a "Self-managing informal internship with Jesus" and began a new journey. I was committed to growing my leadership gift without an external obligation, so I created my own opportunity. When I returned to the US, I am amped. I had already set up a group meeting with curriculum and methodology. I called it 'Leading Ladies Connect' meeting. The meeting happened once month with four ladies. I spent time in prayer for these women, asking for prophetic insight for their lives, then assigning strategy and wisdom from other women of the bible who modeled a parallel experience. It wasn't that I had seen the before, I was simply using what I know; a bible study, prayer and administration. And doing it my way. Personally, the hardest thing about setting up this group was that the participants were my peers. Some ladies in the group were excited and others were confused as to why they were in the group. I didn't have much "governing" authority, they just had to trust and agree to it or not. This wasn't a church related thing; it was simply a me thing. I had an opportunity to express my influence and ran with it. I learned so many lessons from that time and it excites me to see how that very season has evolved to my executive coaching career today. Once you have literally decluttered (purge and organize) your physical space, and metaphorically decluttered your mind (purge lies and organize truth) your boldness to finesse will expand and what seemed like one step becomes the platform for many more.

Strength & Power

To Finesse it, we must know your strengths. Not only do we need to know our strengths, but also believe in them. Self-efficacy refers to our belief about our ability to succeed. The strength-based psychology used by Clifton StrengthsFinder (Buckingham, Clifton Gallup 2001) teaches that our talents and natural abilities should be the focus to produce maximum results. If you desire to know your strength according to Clifton, visit the StrengthsFinders website and take the assessment. The assessment will determine your top 5 strengths and give strategy on implementation It's so easy to focus on our weakness that we can neglect to fuel our strengths due to personal insecurities and a need for control.

Power is such a heavy word. It's a word that we hate to admit we love, but regardless, it's real. Power is the capacity to influence behavior, and while its duty is to secure social welfare of people it's often been used to corrupt society. I believe that power is not the main issue, as it is that lack of power allotted. Biblically speaking, Jesus was very clear (Act 1:8) in stating that we need power, Holy Spirit, to be His witnesses to the world. That power was not for oppression, but spiritual enlightenment and transforming empowerment of others. Lacking to flow is your strengths, which are your god given talents, is a miseducation of true liberation.

According to Whetten and Cameron's textbook on developing management skills, your expertise, attraction, effort and legitimacy are sources of personal power. Expertise is work related knowledge that comes from education, self-directed learning and experience. That partnered with your charisma and appearance can open (or close) more doors than you can imagine. A true commitment and dedication to your expertise is a recipe for maximum influence. While influential people have power, not all powerful people have influence. That's when finesse comes into play. How you handle situations makes all the difference in the outcome.

Let's Chat:

In order to FINESSE it, you must ask yourself, "How can I use what I have access to?" In other words, what's my current capacity? Your ability to finesse (how you handle situations) will be express your influence.

Reflection Questions

1. Do you live an orderly life? When is the last time you purged a room or office?

   _____

   _____

   _____

2. What are your top five strengths and how do you best see these in action?

   _____

   _____

   _____

3. Have you identified your current sphere of influence? If so, how can you be more intentional in leading those individuals.

   _____

   _____

   _____

FLOW WITH IT

Partner with Peace

Write in the king's name whatever pleases you concerning the Jews,
and seal it with the royal signet ring. A document written in the
king's name and sealed with the royal signet ring cannot be revoked.

Esther 8:8

*M*y daughter loves to dance. As of now, I can say she been dancing all her life. When she was eight months old, Chris and I would sing the "Chloe song" and she would wiggle her body side to side. All she had to hear was, "Chlo Chlo… Chlo Chlo… Chlo," and immediately there was movement and laughter as she wiggled and filled us with joy. She loved it so much that we purchased her first drum when she was ten months old. We were amazed at her inclination to music. Now as for me, I wouldn't consider myself a natural dancer. I like to "groove," and I love music, but I am more comfortable and likely to dance when there's an organized movement or dance pattern. Chloe, on the other hand, can just flow with it. When she hears a melody, she moves effortlessly in response.

Flow with Reverence

At our church, we had a dance ministry titled F.L.O.W. This in of itself is a suitable name for a dance team, but it is also an acronym that stands for the "Father Loves Our Worship." The title was inspired by the scripture where David dances until his clothes came off (2 Samuel 6:14). It seemed inappropriate that he would dance like that, but his response to accusations was that he was dancing for the Lord, not for people. Offensive or not, his main objective was to praise and worship the Lord. He was on his second attempt to bring the ark of the covenant back home.

Previously when they journeyed with the ark of God (1 Chronicles 13), he and his team danced, but he did not consult the Lord on how the ark should be handled. What seemed like such a small detail angered the Lord and caused the immediate death of a team player. David was angry because of this situation and almost forfeited the mission completely. I must admit, the Lord's response to this seemed overrated, yet teaches a wealthy lesson. The presence of God is hosted by the consecrated, not the common. To FLOW with it, you must be committed to purifying your soul. Purity arranges for an unhindered flow of communication and movement with the Lord.

> He said to them, 'You are the heads of the Levite families. You and your relatives must consecrate yourselves so that you may bring the ark of the Lord God of Israel to the place I have prepared for it. For the Lord our God burst out in anger against us because you Levites were not with us the first time, for we didn't inquire of him about the proper procedures.'
> -1 Chronicles 15:12-13

The ark of God, also referred to as ark of the covenant was a chest designed as a symbol of the promise (Genesis 12:1-4) that the Lord made with the Israelites. This chest was sacred. God gave very specific instructions for its design. Inside it held the stones of the ten commandments and Aaron's rod. Its cover was also considered the "mercy seat" as the blood of a perfect lamb that had been sacrificed was poured upon it once a year representing atonement for the sins of the people. This was the very manifest presence of the Lord in the old testament. Today, we have a new symbol, the cross. Jesus is the atonement for our sins now and forever. We no longer need to kill an animal to save our souls, we simply have the responsibility to sanctify ourselves. The mission is no longer to carry a box as a symbol, we, ourselves are the symbols. Our decisions, actions and character serve as displays of the ark of the covenant and at this stage of leadership, one cannot afford to move without acknowledging a true praise break. When you Flow with the tangible and weighty presence of God, a misappropriation of authority could cost a life.

Flow with Favor

Managing favor and authority is also like dancing. Authority is delegated powerto influence, and favor is the kindness granted without merit. Esther had favor with the King from the beginning. She was beautiful inside and out, and respectfully submissive to her guardians. After exposing Haman, she was granted authority from the king that moved her to continue to Face it. She now had more responsibility than ever before, yet it was accompanied by favor and authority.

> That same day King Ahasuerus awarded Queen Esther the estate of Haman, the enemy of the Jews. Mordecai entered the king's presence because Esther had revealed her relationship to Mordecai. 2 The king removed his signet ring he had recovered from Haman and gave it to Mordecai, and Esther put him in charge of Haman's estate.
> -Esther 8:1-2

Esther had wisely exposed Haman's plot to the king, but there was still work to be done to secure an opportunity for the Jews to be protected. She appointed Mordecai to be in charge of Haman's house, then proceeded to ask the King to revoke the letters previously commanding the destruction of the Jews. He instructed Mordecai to write a counter-decree authorizing the Jews to defend themselves. I wonder if this request happened with less anxiety for her because she knew she walked in favor. Her request seemed weightier and more cumbersome, but she was able to Flow with it and seize the moment. The authority she gained with words of peace and truth affected 127 provinces and placed a stake in history to be celebrated for generations. Esther used her role as the queen not only to lead, but to provide leadership advancement for others.

> Surely goodness and mercy shall follow me all the days of my life; And I will dwell in the house of the Lord Forever.
> -Psalm 23:6

My friend, Sabrina, uses her influence to advocate for captives of human trafficking and started an organization with the mission to raise awareness and to fund rescue and restoration around the world. During one of our coffee dates, she shared a story with me about preparing her teenage daughter for a homecoming dance. Sabrina's an expert when it comes to taking to teens about relevant topics and specially the topic of sex. Her daughter was quite concerned about the possibility of experiencing a slow dance with boy in his onset of puberty. She needed to know what to do if something awkward and uncomfortable happened. Sabrina responded by saying, "Just always leave room for Jesus, honey."

The essence of Flow with it, is leaving room for Jesus. This is always important, but I am specifically speaking to the chapter in your life where you feel that you are finally on top of things. You are the most comfortable in your skin that you've ever been and enjoying your God-given identity. Making room for Jesus is allowing Him to not only be the DJ who sets the music or makes the decision, but also your lead dancing partner. This dance between you and God is what will sustain your determination. When we are prompted with vision, we must continually listen and lean into the rhythm and rule of the one prompting us. When you Flow with it, you are always leaving room for Jesus to evaluate and redirect.

Flow with Peace

At the end of each year, my husband and I plan some retreat time for one another to reflect, pray and plan. We use this time to get a revelation as to where our focus should be for the next season. One particular year I took away from my retreat time a phrase that revolutionized my pace of life. I said the phrase daily and told all my friends. "I will not live a rushed life," became my anthem. It was such a simple concept, yet it was so challenging. It took me two and a half months to truly stop rushing, although I was declaring it moment after moment. I was at a point in my life where anxiety was following me like a lost puppy. I had a full and active life. On one hand, I just wanted to eat a joy bar and watch Paw Patrol with my children, but after about seven minutes of sitting, I would have a new, innovative idea for our church's leadership structure that I wanted to research. It finally clicked that I was living a rushed life when I found myself doing things contrary to my character. I was arriving at places extra late, I was unprepared for meetings I had scheduled, and maybe for the first time in my life, I could not get organized. Time, structure and order run in my DNA. How did they get lost? I found myself checking my email at traffic lights, and being unusually irritable with my children. One evening while busy at home and my husband asked me, "Why are you rushing?" I could give him no reason. We had no time constraints or sudden deadline. Rushing had become my normal. I scheduled meetings back to back mistaking an adrenaline rush for efficiency.

I had to intentionally reduce my pace. Instead of every moment being a sprint, I needed to run slower, longer. I started by not checking my email at the red light. If I had the urge to check the phone, I called a friend, and told her that I was not living a rushed life. Then I moved to checking my email only on designated days. It was in the time again that I had to remind myself that the time was the Lord's. I only responded to church email on Tuesdays. I instituted a "domestic day" on Wednesdays which is when I cleaned my house did something special with my son. I turned off the notification on my phone and just let a few messages sit unanswered. I knew that March through May would be a busy time of year for us, so when June came, I dedicated seven consecutive weeks to my kids. No impromptu "one-on-ones," no vision casting for the nonprofit, no coaching sessions, not even a discipleship session. It felt so good to live unrushed. When I look back at that year, I realized I had traveled more than I ever had before, I had felt more mature, and life seemed to be the most productive. All because I was able to live with accuracy instead of anxiety. Living an unrushed life does not mean you eliminate ambition or stop pursuing purpose, it simply refers to your pace. Designing clear patterns helped me keep a steady rhythm. Having margin in your life keeps special moment special. It allows for ease in keeping in step with the Holy Spirit. It helps steady the transition in your roles and seasons.

"Busy resting" is a phrase I coined in my first book, *IronDresses: Strength in Femininity.* It's a concept of being busy doing the "good thing," resting. Heavy laden or burdened people are worried or distracted by life's "to do" list. The worry and the distractions keep us from choosing the "good part." If you are living without peace of mind and are constantly under stress, are you choosing the beauty of rest that comes from Christ?" Things get tough, and it seems there is never enough time to get everything done. What seems to be the right thing to do can a distraction or a burden that causes us to miss the opportunities to sit at the feet of Christ. It is important to recognize we still need our beauty rest. When you accepted this invitation for Jesus' yoke, you ultimately signed up for Christ to supply your beauty rest that you might be busy resting. This type of rest is incomparable, and others will notice. They will look at your life and wonder how you do it all. How you balance an active life and look so lovely doing it? As they see what would seem to be "low moments" in your life, they will not be able to disregard the true light that continues to shine, pointing to Christ. You must let them know that you have chosen the "good part," the beauty rest.

To "Flow with it", we must become active and not just busy doing things. Being active is a result of proper assessment and choice. Being busy is having an occupied soul, often with little room for the unexpected. An active life is an engaging soul, in specific pursuit of a known purpose. In the midst of a workout, the trainer may encourage an active rest. This allows your heart rate to descend while your calorie burning continues at a steady rate. Living a rushed life is one full of haste and hurry. When you Flow with peace, you make an exchange for maximum productivity because your pace and space is settled on the presence of God.

Esther did not live a rushed life. She paced with margin. Once she decided to Face it, she found favor from the king and proceeded to Finesse it by using her resources and inviting the king and Haman to first one banquet and then another. My previous rushed-self would not have had the patience to go through planning and attending two banquets. I would have told him everything as soon as I touched the golden scepter. I admire her calm during what seemed so heart-breaking a time. Living unrushed allows the unexpected to become a prop for the miraculous.

> *Yea, though I walk through the valley of the shadow of death, I will fear no evil; For You are with me.*
>
> *-Psalm 23:4*

Flowing with the peace of God is also our banner when we face trials and valleys. I learned this in an intimate way when I experienced a miscarriage. Palms 23 had a new meaning and value. Reading this verse, I always pictured David's journey as he was being hunted by King Saul. It wasn't until I received that unin-vited phone call from the obstetrics nurse informing us that my test results indi-cated a non-viable pregnancy, that the shadow of death seemed within me. My own womb was no longer a place of new life only. The proof of a baby was just a shadow waiting for excretion. This moment paused me for obvious reasons, but simultaneously I felt a peace *over*shadow me. I had time to cry and explore my feelings, but sadness had limited opportunity because I was already full and living a life in which I was grateful for all that God has done for me. .

I wonder if Mary, the mother of Jesus, felt like this when she tried to explain her virgin pregnancy to others (Luke 1:30-38). I had to explain death in my womb, and she had to convince that the life in her womb was not a result of betrayal that warranted her lawful death. The death that was waiting to be addressed in both circumstances were overshadowed by the Lord's presence. I con-sider myself privileged to have had a dream about my unborn child shortly after receiving the bad news. This dream was so sacred and vivid that it was difficult to separate reality. It was nothing I asked for or even knew that I needed, but it was an unforgettable experience that solidified my upward movement from the valley. I was certain that God was with me and that purpose and meaning would grow from this. Joseph, Mother Mary's husband, had a dream as well, and similarly, the revelation prompted his loyalty and next moves as he was assured that this baby was a fulfillment of something greater. (Matt 1:20-25)

The hardest part of for me was explaining the loss to others. I didn't' really have answers for their questions, and I couldn't control the emotions it would trigger within them. I remember a specific instance months later when I needed to break the news to a friend at the gym. I forgot that she even knew I was pregnant until she commended my workout endurance considering my "pregnancy". It was awkward to have to say, "Thank you, but by the way, I am no longer pregnant due to a miscarriage." After explaining, there was five seconds of silence that felt like eternity, but after the pause she disclosed that she's had six miscarriages. Here we are, about to start this workout class and this woman is unintentionally standing vulnerable. I shared with her what I knew to be true, that God is the only giver of life, and I expressed my gratitude for Jesus as redeemer. I am not sure how it all connected with her situation, but it seemed like a breath of fresh air. She explained how it gave perspective to the lingering question she had during her span of tragedy. The presence of God was so strong, and was yet another glimpse of how flowing with the peace is contagious and fruitful even in what seems like barren seasons.

Let's Chat:

Partnering with peace is a continuum of reverencing the presence of God, embracing a space for favor to flow, and allowing purpose to overshadow every situation, good or bad. Your pace is sometimes reflective of who you trust, and your actions are a billboard for the authority you walk in. As leaders, let's never surrender to anxiety, but press into the authority provided for us to flow with it.

> Do not be anxious about anything, but in every situation, by prayer and petition, with thanksgiving, present your requests to God. And the peace of God, which transcends all understanding, will guard your hearts and your minds in Christ Jesus.
>
> -Phil 4:6-7

Reflection Questions: How to Partner with Peace

1. What areas in your life do you seem to have favor? What authority has been given to you? How are you maximizing those opportunities?

   _____

   _____

   _____

2. List the patterns or consistencies in your leadership that may be a distraction for your growth in the next season.

   _____

   _____

   _____

3. Are you living a rushed life? If so, how can you prioritize and pace your life with margin?

   _____

   _____

   _____

CONCLUSION

Final Thought

*On the third day, Esther dressed in her royal clothing and
stood in the inner courtyard of the palace facing it.*

Esther 5:1

The book of Esther is the case study that provided the six strategies of this
book. Esther 5:1, is the focal verse in which the title itself is derived. When
I read it, I'm reminded of Jesus' crucifixion and resurrection. Jesus knew that
offering His life as a sacrifice on the cross was the only way to atone for our sin.
He endured and died on the cross and was buried in the grave. He "faced it."
Three days later, Jesus Himself changed his cloths, stood out of the grave and
"faced it." His character, confidence and competence were confirmed at that point
and eternal contributions were deposited. Because Jesus embraced His leadership
inheritance, the old covenant was fulfilled, and a new law was birthed, making us
joint heirs with the Messiah.

> For you did not receive the spirit of bondage again to fear, but you
> received the Spirit of adoption by whom we cry out, 'Abba, Father.' The
> Spirit Himself bears witness with our spirit that we are children of God,
> and if children, then heirs—heirs of God and joint heirs with Christ, if
> indeed we suffer with Him, that we may also be glorified together.
> -Romans 8:15-17

My hope is that you revisit these six strategies often for growth. These six
strategies to leverage your leadership potential will be a timeless tool for leadership
success.

My children and future generations were a major motivation to complete
this book.

I desire to enhance awareness by shining light on the truth that we are more, can do more and have more opportunity for greatness than most of us live in daily. As Esther was, we are living in a world of conflict in culture. Women and men are being persecuted, literally and mentally based on false contracts and we are spreading those beliefs to generations like germs.

In the book of Esther there were critical problems present. We discover that there was a decree written (Esther 3:13) to destroy, kill and annihilate all the Jews in the kingdom, simply because of a personal matter - pride. These laws were made based on selfish gain and situational power rather than justice and commonwealth. There was a law that suggest the death penalty for anyone who approached the king without invitation. The law hindered Esther's actions. The law is limiting to her purpose, ultimately blocking a generational blessing. The previous Queen was fired because she did not comply with the king's summons. The ruler punished her to make a statement to other women. Although the scripture says that she was already beautiful and good-looking, she had a year of treatment to her body to be up to the king's standard of physical appearance. The only preparation for this position needed was that which pleased him. The King considered her the "better" one, replacing Vashti.

There are many issues in this passage of scripture that we are still thwarting us today. We can get caught up in pleasing those around us more than the God above us. This results in a downgrade of uniqueness. The view we have of ourselves does not match our true design. We are not merely templates of pleasure; we are temples of the presence. The ultimate question is this: Whose lenses matter most? What narrative are you going to believe and dispense? That of current culture, or of your creator?

God graciously gave us a solution to the problems, you. Don't forget that the name of this book of the bible is "Esther;" not because she wrote it, but because she was God's solution. Could it be that her whole life was preserved for this moment? From orphan to queen was not just her *come up* story, it was the *setup* for her to walk in purpose. She could not wait on a solution because she was the solution. When Esther aligns with her actual identity, she's able to see her greater purpose. Her preparation is no longer based on her fleeting exterior, rather her personal spiritual growth.

Therefore, we are ambassadors for Christ, since God is making his appeal through us. We plead on Christ's behalf: 'Be reconciled to God.'
-2 Corinthians 5:20

Similarly, could God be calling you to be the very solution to the trouble in the world? Yes! God is pleading with us. Just He did with Esther, God is suggesting that it's our time. It's time to put on your royal clothing, take a stand and FACE it. It's time to embrace your leadership inheritance and thrive.

ABOUT THE AUTHOR

*W*ife, mother, author, entrepreneur, educator, and lover of Jesus, Cherelle Johnson is the creator and founder of IronDresses Inc. IronDresses Inc. is a 501(c)3 organization dedication to women's empowerment with programs such as The Glam Squad and Dream Girls, with a goal to impact, influence, and inspire excellence for women in leadership. Cherelle has hosted annual women's conferences in which the focus encompasses all facets of womanhood including how to maximize your season as: mother, daughter, sister, and wife.

A double alumna of James Madison University, Cherelle holds a Bachelor's degree in Business Administration as well as a Master's degree in Science of Education in AHRD. In 2013, Cherelle authored her first book titled IronDresses: Strength in Femininity and this publication became the very framework for the birth of her now current organization.

Between her current work as an Adjunct Instructor and Executive Coach, Cherelle is married to Pastor Chris Johnson Sr., Founder and Lead Pastor of Divine Unity Community Church and a mother to their three children Chloe Madison, Christopher Jr. and Caleb Z. With her husband, Cherelle has traveled nationally and internationally training and equipping leaders.